Living in Two Worlds

Contents

Features

Have you ever heard of an animal that leads a double life? Turn to page 5 for more about amphibians.

Long-legged lizards are racing on water! Turn to page 9 to discover more about the lizards that can stand on their own two feet.

Is it a joke? What mammal has the bill of a duck and the body of an otter? Find out more in **Trick or Truth?** on page 20.

Just how far can a person dive underwater? Discover how technology helps deep-sea divers in **How Low Can You Go?** on page 25.

What can you tell from a turtle's shell?

Visit **www.pearsoned.ca/inquizitive**
for more about **TURTLES.**

Living in Two Worlds

Many of the world's most interesting creatures live in two worlds—in water and on land.

Many of these creatures are **amphibians**. Some are **reptiles**. Others are **mammals** that spend time in the water looking for food. Some birds and insects also spend their lives both in water and on land.

1 Dragonflies lay their eggs in water.

The word *amphibian* comes from the Greek word *amphibios*, which means "a being with a double life."

5 The new dragonflies fly away.

Life Cycle of Dragonflies

4 The new dragonflies dry their wings in the sun.

3 After a while the nymphs climb out of the water. They break out of their old skin. Now they are dragonflies.

2 The young are called **nymphs**. They can take several weeks to hatch.

Frogs and Toads

Frogs and toads are amphibians. Amphibians cannot live far from a watery environment. Like most amphibians, frogs and toads lay their eggs in water. Tadpoles hatch from the eggs. Each **larva** looks like a little fish with a long tail. It takes in oxygen through its gills. Later it develops lungs and breathes air. The tadpoles grow and change until they can live on land as well as in the water.

Don't Be Fooled

Most toads are lumpy and bumpy. They have short legs. Most frogs are smooth and have long legs.

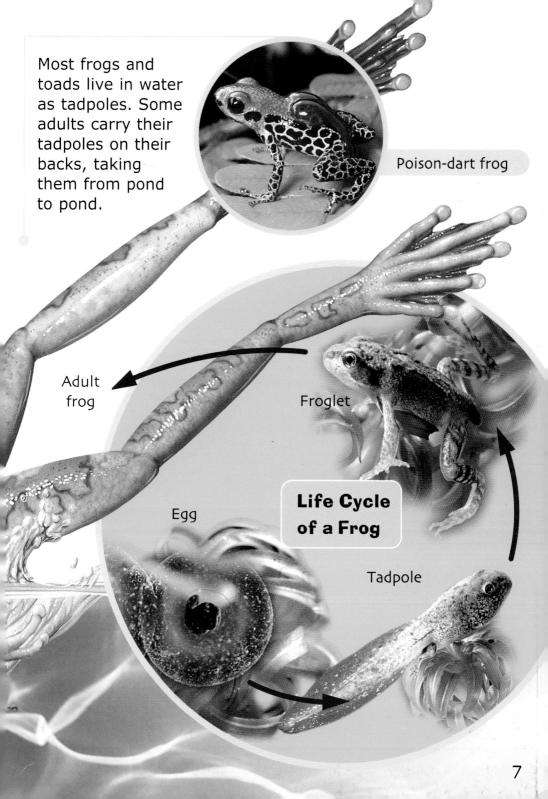

Most frogs and toads live in water as tadpoles. Some adults carry their tadpoles on their backs, taking them from pond to pond.

Poison-dart frog

Adult frog

Froglet

Egg

Life Cycle of a Frog

Tadpole

Lizards

Lizards are reptiles. Many reptiles live on land and in water. Many lizards live near fresh water. Some search for insects in the plants that grow beside rivers and lakes. Some jump into the water to escape their enemies.

The marine iguana is the only lizard that spends time in the ocean. It dives under waves to eat plants that grow on rocks by the seashore.

South America

Marine iguanas live on the Galapagos Islands. These islands are home to many unusual and wonderful animals.

Central
America

The basilisk lizard from
Central America runs across
the water on its long legs. It
has scaly fringes on its back
toes that keep it from sinking.

Crocodilians lay their eggs in a nest and cover them for warmth. These reptiles guard their nests and scare away predators.

Crocodilians can crawl.

Crocodilians Up Close

Crocodilians have thick, scaly skin to keep them safe. Their webbed toes and long, swishing tails help them move quickly through the water. Their powerful jaws and strong, sharp teeth help them snatch and kill their prey.

Crocodilians may be fierce creatures, but the female looks after her eggs and young more than most reptiles. A mother and her young often stay together for many weeks until the hatchlings can look after themselves.

A female alligator will carry her hatchlings in her mouth to a pond, where she will look after them.

Crocodilians

Crocodiles and alligators belong to a family of reptiles called **crocodilians**. Crocodilians are some of the world's largest and most dangerous reptiles. They can float easily in water and drift slowly towards their **prey**. This helps them save their energy for a surprise attack!

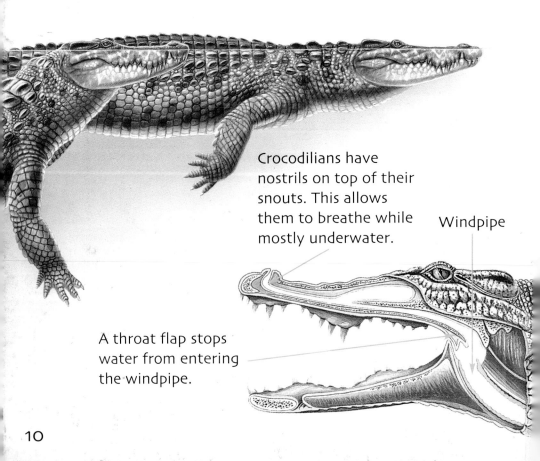

Crocodilians have nostrils on top of their snouts. This allows them to breathe while mostly underwater.

Windpipe

A throat flap stops water from entering the windpipe.

Crocodiles and alligators live in warm, swampy countries around the world. American alligators often hunt around waterbird nesting sites. An alligator can leap from the water to catch a young bird.

Don't Be Fooled

Alligator

When an alligator's mouth is closed, you can see its top teeth only. An alligator has a wide snout.

Crocodile

When a crocodile's mouth is closed, you can see its top teeth and some of its bottom teeth. It has a narrower snout.

Crocodilians do not use their legs much for swimming. Instead, they use their long, strong tails as paddles to move through water.

Crocodilians can gallop.

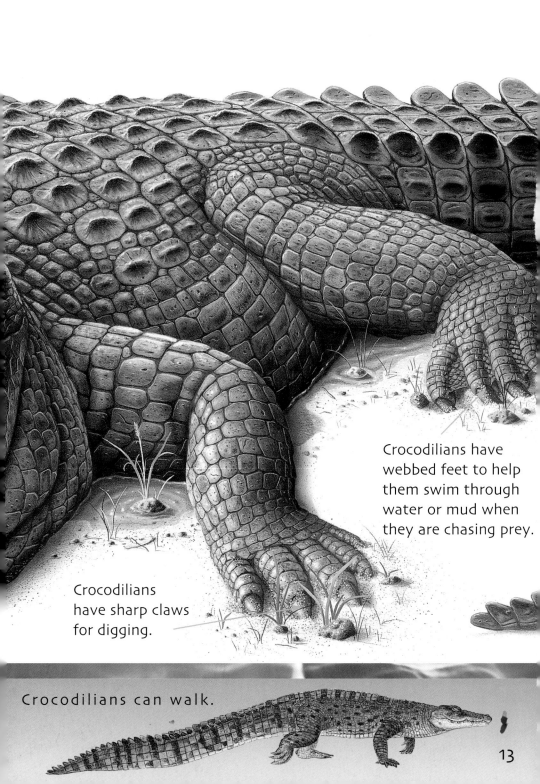

Crocodilians have webbed feet to help them swim through water or mud when they are chasing prey.

Crocodilians have sharp claws for digging.

Crocodilians can walk.

Turtles

Turtles are reptiles too. Many turtles live both on land and in water. Most turtles come to the surface of the water to breathe air, but some turtles can also take in oxygen from the water.

Most freshwater turtles lay their eggs in soil or in sand. They hunt on land as well as in the water. Turtles' shells help to protect them. Most turtles can pull their heads into their shells if they are in danger.

What can you tell from a turtle's shell?
Visit **www.pearsoned.ca/inquizitive**
for more about **TURTLES.**

SITESEEING · PLANTS & ANIMALS ·

16

Neck
that can
pull head
in and out

Upper
shell

Outer layer,
called scutes

Turtles are the
only reptiles
with a shell.

Lower shell

The snapping
turtle has a
bright red
tongue. It uses
its tongue to lure
fish to its mouth.

Furry Swimmers

Many mammals live in and out of water. Beavers, otters, and raccoons live in or near water. Some of these furry swimmers have webbed feet and a special coat to keep them warm.

Some of these animals even build their homes in the water. Beavers fell trees with their huge front teeth. They use the trunks and branches to make homes, called lodges, in the water.

Freshwater otters live along rivers, streams, and lakes in many parts of the world. They are expert swimmers and divers.

Raccoons live in North America. They hunt in pools and streams for frogs and fish.

Where beavers live

Trick or Truth?

A gift from a faraway land has all sorts of Londoners mystified!

In 1798, a stuffed platypus was sent from Australia to England. The people there had never seen a platypus before. They thought it was a trick. They thought someone had stitched the bill of a duck to the body of an otter!
Was it trick or truth?

Strange but True!

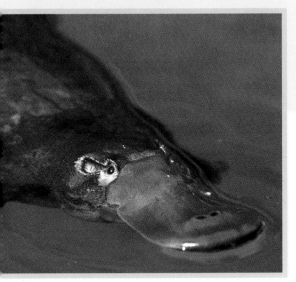

The platypus may seem a bit mixed up, but it is for real. It has a bill like a duck's and webbed feet for swimming. It is furry and about as big as a cat. It is a mammal, but it lays eggs. Baby platypuses drink their mother's milk.

Platypuses live in Australia. They dig burrows in the banks of streams. The burrows are usually underwater. The platypus is perfectly suited to living in and out of water.

The eyes and ears of the platypus are in a special groove that closes when the animal is underwater.

When on land, the platypus can fold back the webs on its front feet so it can use its claws to walk and dig.

Sea Mammals

Sea lions are sea mammals. They are expert swimmers. Although they spend much time at sea, they come back to shore to have their babies, called pups. Sea lions can move well on land.

Hundreds of sea lions gather on rocky coasts in large groups called colonies. They bark, grunt, and bellow at each other.

Most sea lions live in the northern part of the world. They hunt for food such as fish, squid, and octopus in seaweed forests.

Walruses are sea mammals. They can pull themselves up onto land with their long, strong tusks.

Taking the Plunge

People also spend a lot of time in water. They swim, fish, and dive. They like to explore coral reefs and kelp forests in search of fish and other sea life. People may not have special ear or throat flaps, but they have invented many things to help them survive for long periods of time in a watery world.

Scuba diver

WORD BUILDER

The word *scuba* is made up from the first letter of five different words: **s**elf-**c**ontained **u**nderwater **b**reathing **a**pparatus.

How Low Can You Go?

From simple masks to complex diving suits, tanks, and underwater equipment, technology allows people to explore underwater worlds to depths of 11 kilometres below the surface.

Glossary

amphibian – a cold-blooded animal that lives part of its life in water and part on land. Frogs, toads, and salamanders are amphibians.

crocodilian – the name for the family of large reptiles that includes alligators and crocodiles

larva – the young, worm-like form of an animal that must grow and change a lot before it looks like its parents

mammal – an animal that feeds its young on mother's milk. Mammals are warm-blooded and are the only animals that have hair.

nymph – the newly-hatched form of some insects. A nymph must go through major body changes before it looks like an adult.

prey – an animal that is hunted and eaten by another animal

reptile – a cold-blooded animal that crawls on its belly or creeps on short legs. All reptiles have dry, scaly skin.

Index

Larva
(tadpole)

Adult
(frog)

Discussion Starters

1 How is a turtle different from other reptiles? How does a turtle use its shell? What are the different parts of the shell? Why might some turtles be endangered?

2 Crocodilians have a bad reputation with many people. Why might this be? What reasons would crocodilians have for behaving in ways that appear cruel to people? How are humans cruel to crocodiles and alligators?

3 Many creatures can be described as amphibians. Why? Name some amphibians you know.